Singing Birds and Silence

A Collection of Poems

from

Janet Wilkes

janetwilkes1947@gmail.com

Published in 2022 by
Arthur H Stockwell Ltd
West Wing Studios
Unit 166, The Mall
Luton, Bedfordshire
ahstockwell.co.uk

British Library Cataloguing-in-Publication
Data: A catalogue record for this book is
available from the British Library.
ISBN 9781399918893

Second Edition 2022

In memory of my lovely husband, Keith

Also my parents, Fred and Margaret Handisyde

Royalties from the sale of this book
will be donated to
Blesma, The Limbless Veterans
115 New London Road
Chelmsford
Essex
CM2 0QT

Contents

Foreword

"Leave the whole matter in the hands of God"
—Eugene De Mazenod

This book of poetry takes me to some beautiful places as Janet shares with us her love of words. She shares something precious and alive, colourful and spiritual and it is inspiring.

Father Raymond Warren, OMI

Director
De Mazenod House Retreat and Spirituality Centre
London, E1 8BL

A Note from the Author

Dear Reader,

In this short anthology I hope there is something that will resonate with an experience you have had or with somewhere that you've been.

I hope you will find as much pleasure in reading these poems as I have had in writing them.

Poetry is the way we express our thoughts with the finest words we know and the way the ancients spoke to God.

There are many forms of writing poetry and anyone can do it. All you need to do is take a pen and describe the place you're in, either where you are or in your thoughts. If it's a happy place the lines will flow.

I hope this little book will give you comfort and every blessing.

Janet

Singing Birds
and Silence

Let There Be Light

In the beginning was nothing,
Nothing, nothing at all, but God
Said "Let there be light" and there was.
God formed man from the dust of the
Earth (his skin tone taking the shade
Of the clay from which he was hewn)
And a wife – yet there is more to
That tale, so we won't go there now.

Four thousand years later Saint Paul
Reminded people that God said,
"Let light shine out of darkness."
And we remind ourselves now in
The autumn, when we celebrate
Eid, Diwali, Rosh Hashanah,
That at every fall we need
Light and a Day of Thanksgiving.

Genesis 1:3
2 Corinthians 4:6

Wild Wet Wasteland

Beyond the wild wet wasteland's thicket
There was a garden facing eastwards
Filled with flowers, rosemary, rue, roots
For pulling, fruits for picking; but the
Fruit on the tree in the middle of
The garden was the Landlord's. "Don't eat,"
He said. But the young couple did. Then
One day they took wing and flew away.

Was it youth or ignorance or pride
That led us, when young, so far away
Or were we just misadvised before
We were wafted on sultry air to
Hard places where God showed us what life
Was like for many people – hungry,
Dispossessed and alone – beyond the
Eastern cherubim that guard Eden?

Now we need gardens more than ever
To reflect, relax and recover—
To return to paradise and to
Be home in Eden. To be alone.
To think about our journeying and
What caused the sudden expulsion from
All we knew and about returning
To the same old familiar place.

Beyond the driveway and wooden fence
The gated entrance and 'PRIVATE' sign,
There's a garden and pagoda tree
Beneath whose floral hanging clusters
Residents sit and muse in almost
Incoherent words on distant days
About their youth and ignorance and
Pride when they took wing – and flew away.

Genesis 2:8–9

Homecoming

Can we go back where we belong—
Familiar scenes, likely places,
Whose auras remind us of times when
We were happy, when we felt safe, and
Where, in whimsy, we would go again?
Can we go back there? Would that be good?
Would the old be gone, the new be cold?
Would seeing it now spoil the idyll?
Would the memories scupper and fade?
Or could we see, with greater clarity,
Places where, years ago, we were from?

The Final Mile

Here on earth, Lord, You carried a Cross
On which the whole world's sins were laid but
In sight of Calv'ry you fell beneath
The load on dusty ground and Roman
Soldiers, having a job to do, seized
A pilgrim and, in front of his sons,
Forced him to shoulder the cross and to
Go through noisy streets of frolicking
Festival-goers, leering, jeering
And shouting insults as You walked the
Final mile. He didn't know You Lord.
He was there for Passover. But what
He did "for the least of these my brethren,"
He did for You.

Matthew 25:40

Iona

Come to this sacred island where
Prayers are offered and God is
Sought. This thin place beyond the edge
Where heaven almost touches earth.
Here in the hush of the morning
Before light rises in the East,
Before the mist clears and the voice
Of a lone dove is heard calling,
The dreaming ends and one hears sounds
Of water slapping on the shore
And shingle slipping with the ebb
And one knows there IS a God who
Cares and Jesus said, "This day you
Will be with me in Paradise."

Luke 23:43

Heatwave

Lord, we are in Your hands tonight.
The blistering sun that slowed our
Work, parched the grass and dried the soil
So solid that even water
Couldn't penetrate to the roots
Of plants that shrivelled at high noon.

We want an end to the heatwave
(though grateful for the warmth and sun)
And petition a gentle breeze,
And a cooler day tomorrow.

Yet if tomorrow brings no rain
We must be our own well-watered
Garden. We must turn our wastelands
Into Eden and make deserts
Bloom where joy and gladness shall be
Found, thanksgiving and sounds of praise.

Isaiah 51:3

Candyfloss and Seagulls

At the end of a perfect day give thanks
For the warmth of the sun and the sound of
The seashells shifting as each wave recedes
Before another line of white spume is
Lifted and dispersed 'long the cobbled beach.
For harbour smells of lobster pots mingling
With the tang each tide's seaweed brings from the
Ocean. For candyfloss, ice-cream parlours
And the spectacle of seagulls swooping
To snatch food from the laps of astonished
Visitors who, when their coaches leave, will
Always say, "It's been a wonderful day."
So, as you go, give thanks to God. Give thanks.
At the end of a perfect day – give thanks.

The Ocean Floor

Hewn stones are profane, but those sunk
Deep on the ocean floor, moulded
By tides (whose long green foliage
Feeds the hungry in this wat'ry
Desert), stand like altars in this
Wilderness. It's a lonely place—
Awesome, dark and silent – where no
Man dare sink so low and none can
Fathom why fishes lurk or why
In this eerie place there is a
Luminance from their scales and eyes
Illuminating coral swathes.
What is their work here? What is their
Purpose? Why are they swishing and
Swooshing all day long? What *is* this
Dark, fathomless, cavernous depth,
This deep limbo where no man goes?
It is another world we share
Our planet with. The ocean floor
Where other continents exist.

Psalm 95:4

Morecambe Bay

God gathered water into one
Place. He called the dry land earth and
He made rivers flow to the sea.
In estuaries, when tides are
Low, we pray for night workers and
Those who know nothing of quicksands
And fast incoming rushing waves
(For the bright lights on the farther
Side of the eight-mile bay are all
They see as they gather cockles.)

We pray too for those journeying
From busy city streets, who don't
Expect to find, among sedge grass,
Deep gullies and salt marshes. For
They come to watch gulls skim water
And pick sea lavender, before
Returning to tenements in
Urban landscapes, far from the sea
And the wind and the sky and the
White misty salt-tanged ocean air.

*Remembering the Morecambe Bay cockling disaster in February
2004, when twenty-three Chinese cockle-pickers drowned. They
were trapped by a rising tide and swept out to sea.*

Tom

"It's only a scratch," said Tom, yet I'm still
Here, still able to wheel myself round and
See others that I'm told are worse than me
And remember, with crystal clarity,
Rorking carrions above the clearing
Smoke and feel their wings flap-splatting in the
Blood. "Get off!" I yelled. "I'm still here. I'm not
Done yet. I have a home, wife and children
And when I get back I have things to do."
But this vulture fixed me with his evil
Eye, daring me to call another shot.
I wanted to swipe him, but my arm had
Gone; to kick him, but I had no legs; to
Tell him war should never be his banquet,
But I was overcome with tiredness…
Then smoke swirled round as incense and I saw
In this wilderness a serpent lifted
High like a talisman round a pole and
I saw angels, hundreds of them, thousands,
And I called out, "God, I'm not ready yet."
Then they lifted me from the bed to the
Wheelchair. "It's only a scratch," the Sergeant
Said. "Don't worry. It's Church Parade now. You
Relax. Let us get on and sort this out."

All Will Be Well

After too long in that bleak place I
Moved. It was as if the tide had turned.
I was in a friendlier place, not
Slipping back with every step I took.
Along The common horse chestnuts bloomed,
Apples blossomed and the scent of spring,
And the smell of polished floors in an
Old well-lived-in house, where the floorboards
Creaked and the windows rattled, gave a
Reassurance that all will be well.

All shall be well and all manner
of thing shall be well"

Julian of Norwich 1342-1416

London Sunset

How many suns smile as they set,
Glowing with pride as they sink down
To a line on the sky where they
Disappear for the night, leaving
Curtains half drawn on those who, work
Done, head home neath the dark'ning sky?

Across the Thames (always in the
West) either circling Parliament
Or the London Eye, depending
On the time of year, without fail
This friendly face comes, sooner in
Winter, to say "Goodnight. God bless."

Advent

Advent is cold with sharp winds, short
Days and penitence and each year
The pink candle in the Advent
Wreath gets nicked and somebody goes
To Poundland for another one.
But it's time to remember God
Breathed life into Adam's lungs and,
At Nazareth, told Mary that
She would conceive and bear a Child.

And *we* can conceive in this world
Things we hope for and can find strength
In memories of those who've gone
Before us and companionship
With people who reach out to us
As we wait at the darkest time
Of the year, when the sun is at
Its lowest, for Christ to be born.

Luke 1:26–31

Christmas

When Christ was born Mary and Joseph were away from home with nowhere to sleep and shared their space with animals and farming implements. Later His life was sought and they had to flee to another country.

It's a time of mixed emotions, but I like to remember the happy times long ago, when we had nothing, when my parents, by using their wit and imagination, were able to make Christmas warm and festive.

Sunday-School Party, 1953

I remember that Christmas party,
Scoffing sandwiches, cakes and meringues
On trestle tables awash with squash
(Orange and lemon) and playing blind
Man's bluff. And the team game
When the beanbag got stuck on a ledge
High on the wall so the girls' team won.

We were spoilt little brats, but Sunday
School was a wholesome diversion when
There was no telly and shops were shut.
And the teachers' pantomime was an
Absolute wow with dear Miss Bennett
Overplaying her part as a maid
In an apron and little black dress.

Yes, it was memorable. How could
Anything like that be repeated?
The atmosphere was right. Rationing
Had ended and the war was over.
Rebuilding had begun and we were
All looking forward to a future
and Christmas, when Jesus would be born.

Robin

The robin comes at Christmas time
Red-breasted, cheerful, chirruping,
To deck the halls, hang the holly,
Singing, "It's Christmas now."

He pecks the berries, tweaks the leaves,
Flitters and twitters and flutters
His wings. So sing, little Robin.
Just sing and be happy.

At Easter as he loosed Christ's thorns
His coat was torn and stained with blood.
So let him wear his bloodstained coat.
It's Christmas – be happy.

Stay Here With Us

There are things I can do in the
Dark – reach out to you, wherever
You are – talk to you – hold your hand.
These are things I do for my friends—
Whoever, wherever you are.
When erroneous assumptions
Are made and falsehoods are written
In 'authoritative reports',
Dear Friend, don't go to that dark place.
Some have sought that eerie pasture
And angels have already left
Their shining on barks of trees and
Spirits skim the water. Dear Friend,
Don't venture there. It's Christmas now—
Dear Friend, don't go – stay here with us.

Stable Sanctuary

On Christmas Eve animals
Made ready for guests in their
Cold, dark, draughty stable.
In every inn beds were
Aired, steps were swept and by night-
Fall all rooms were taken.
Then a pregnant girl on a
Donkey, finding no room left
That night, gave birth in a
Stable and laid her Baby
In a manger full of hay
While animals stood round.
Had anything like this happened before?
Had animals in shelters and stables
Ever opened their doors at midnight
And given their space or bedding, feeding
Troughs, food or shelters in the dark in the
Cold as a sanctu'ry, to God, on earth?

Were Shepherds Needed?

Were shepherds needed at the birth
When summoned late one night to go
In haste to Bethlehem, where a
Young woman had arrived and had
Suddenly gone into labour?
"Fear not," the angel said. "I bring
Tidings of joy – a Saviour comes."
And they found Christ in an outhouse
Where animals slept and hay was
Stored and the chickens clucked and plucked
The straw from bales around the walls.

Was this the promised Saviour
Foretold by prophets long ago?
And were the shepherds needed there
Because they would make known what they'd
Been told concerning this Child and—
Like paparazzi – spread the news
Over the town of Bethlehem?

Luke 2:17

Hoping

I have not come like a shepherd,
Wit-scared at night to offer help
With nothing but myself. I have
Come laden with this moment's cares—
Mem'ries of Christmas long ago—
Hoping *this* year will be happy,
That the meal will go well, people
Will get on – that the bereaved, the
Divorced and the jobless among
Us can, for one day, remember
The dangerous road Mary trod
To Bethlehem and the manger
Where she placed her Baby and those
Among us who still have nothing.

When the Sun Hung Low

In a cold stable, a couple, tired from
Their journey, lay down with animals. It
Was the eve of the Saturnalian
Feast Rome celebrated to mark the
Winter solstice – the shortest day – when the
Sun hung low and the men emulated
The God Saturn (the Sower) by lighting
Windows in their homes and scattering seeds.

But in 4 BC the stable was dark.
Only in the corners candles flickered.
There would be no honky-tonk, no dancing,
No ginger snaps, honey buns nor front doors
Decorated with deep-red-berried wreaths.
This Solstice would be marked by a newborn
Child on whom Orient kings and shepherds
would gaze in wonder, wide-eyed and speechless.
Later the Emperor Constantine would
Call it the Nativity of Christ.

*The seven day Feast of Saturnalia began on 17th December of
the Julian calendar to honour the agricultural God Saturn*

It's Cold Outside

It's cold outside, so come into
The stable and see the baby
"What baby?" you ask.
"This shelter is for animals.
In this draughty shed for cattle
With hay for the cows

It's cold outside, so just come in,
Shut the door and come and kneel down
beside the manger.
"For He shall be called the Son of
The Highest and of His kingdom
There shall be no end."

Luke 1:32–33

Light from the Star

Hundreds of camels came from the east
In elegant lines across the sand
With Orient kings carrying gold
Trav'lling by night following a star,
Resting in inns where talk of new kings
Made Herod stir deeply in his sleep.

Then it stopped at an unlikely spot.
This was no inn, no home – no place for
A baby to be born – yet the light
From the star shone like a laser on
The stable where Christ, with Mary, lay
Helpless, homeless, hunted by Herod.

Matthew 2:9 and 13

Out of Egypt

Joseph sensed trouble was ahead. From
The moment three men were helped down from
Their camels, shielding their eyes from light
From the star, they had been reticent
About meeting Herod. Surely when
Kings meet each other they smile, but these
Persian kings turned their camels around
And returned home by another way.

Violence happens when one doesn't
Know how to handle suffering, when
One finds no road and routes lead only
To hazardous swathes of dark terrain
And rutted ground filled with twisted wire.
As when Herod (on hearing Christ was
Born), feared a new king would depose him
And, on hearing the wise men had tricked
Him, became violent and ordered that
All young boys in Bethlehem be killed.

Then Joseph, unable to sleep that
Night, hastily saddled his donkey
And, from his window, the innkeeper
Saw them go south towards Egypt, far
Beyond the farthest star, where they would
Remain until news of Herod's death
To fulfill the ancient prophecy,
"Out of Egypt have I called My Son."

Matthew 2:12–16

24

Rahab

Rahab, the harlot, has not been
Airbrushed from history. Her creedal
Statement "The Lord your God indeed
Is God in heaven above and
On earth below" made certain she
Would be commended in scripture
For giving sanctuary to
The spies whom Joshua sent to
Jericho – then foiling the King's
Men who came searching for them and
Directing them another way.
Now, with just three other women,
Tamar, Ruth, her daughter-in-law
(A widow from Moab and a
Foreigner), who foraged for food
Around the edges of a field,
And Bathsheba, Uriah's wife,
She's mentioned in Matthew's Gospel's
Genealogy of Jesus.

Matthew 1:5

Singing Birds and Silence

Singing birds and silence remind me of
Christmas long ago with coal fires, candles,
Sweet chestnuts, crackers and a pine tree that
Scented the room and shed needles on the
Brown linoleum that covered the floor.

We put cotton wool on its branches to
Look like snow and made little lanterns from
Toilet rolls and a star from two equi-
Lateral triangles, painted yellow.

After Christmas it went back outside, back
Into the heavy London clay that was
Our garden. It liked it there where it grew
A little taller each year that passed and
Greener with the silence and singing birds.

The Table

A woman filled with gratitude this morning
Put her tea tray on the table.
Outside – barely visible – was the garden she'd created.
The flowers had gone, but there were still green leaves.
"I'm alive," she thought, "and grateful for all of this."
She sipped her tea and, as the morning air drew back
The curtains of the night, she became more conscious
Of the long journey she'd had
To reach this point of leisurely morning rising.
She placed on the table the rush and scrum
She used to have to leave her home to go to work.
She placed there too the 'standing only' in crowded trains,
The acne that needed camouflaging, the stockings she used to mend,
And the lunches, long ago, that were only sandwiches filled with paste.
She put them also on the table.
Then she said, "I survived."
And looking back, long after their paths diverged,
She saw, sprinkled along the way like stardust,
Luminaries – people who'd been kind, pleasant and affable—
Those who were wise and gave direction,
Who would never have known how far their words would go—
And put them on the table.
Then she remembered her lovely husband and put him on the table too,
With her neighbours and her friends,
And thanked God for all He'd done for her.
Then lastly she picked up the rekindled relationship with her sister.
Their relationship went back further than them all—
Right back to the beginning, with shared meals, memories and clothes.
She had always been there—
And she put that on the table.

Also from Janet Wilkes

AFTER THE BLOSSOM

Janet Wilkes

MY STORY

Lightning Source UK Ltd.
Milton Keynes UK
UKHW012318270922
409528UK00001B/2